An INCREDIBLE JOURNEY

THE STORY OF ALCOCK AND BROWN

BY *CAROLYN SLOAN*
ILLUSTRATED BY SIMON SMITH

Silver Burdett Press
Parsippany, New Jersey

• INTRODUCTION •

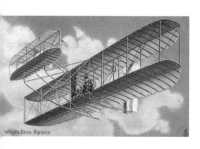

Wright.Bros.Biplane

The Wright brothers designed and made bicycles before building airplanes. Their first successful plane, Flyer 1, was a flimsy machine made from wood, cloth, and wire. However, their first attempt to fly it under power, on December 14, 1903, failed when Wilbur Wright took off and then crashed into the sand.

In 1913, *The Daily Mail* offered a prize of £10,000 ($50,000) for the first nonstop flight across the Atlantic. It was a joke to most people. Fly across 2,000 miles (3,200 km) of ocean? Impossible!

But Lord Northcliffe, the editor of *The Daily Mail*, was deadly serious. He had visions of regular transatlantic flight. He looked into the future and could imagine London morning newspapers on sale in the streets of New York that same evening.

Ten years earlier, on December 17, 1903, he had watched two American brothers, Orville and Wilbur Wright, make the first powered flight over a stretch of sand at Kitty Hawk, North Carolina. Before this, people had tried to fly—in balloons, kites, airships—all of which are lighter than air. The Wright brothers' flying machine, *Flyer 1*, proved that heavier-than-air flight was possible.

Flyer 1 was a strange contraption—more like a bicycle than a plane, really. The Wright brothers made it by fitting an engine to a biplane glider and using bicycle chains and gears to drive the two propellers. The pilot lay on his stomach across the lower wing and controlled the aircraft by wires and levers. It flew a distance of 120 feet (37 meters).

Meanwhile in Europe all sorts of weird flying machines were being tried out. *The Daily Mail* at that time offered a £1,000 ($5,000) prize to anyone who could fly across the English Channel.

Frenchman Louis Blériot took up this challenge. It took great courage to fly over open sea in a plane that could not be guaranteed to fly for more than 40 minutes. Blériot did it in July 1909—overtaking the ship that steamed along below to escort him.

In 1913, when *The Daily Mail* announced its Atlantic challenge, the technology to attempt the 2,000-mile (3,200-km) flight did not exist. But the enthusiasm to develop it certainly did.

The following year saw the outbreak of World War I. Pilots and flying machines were now in demand. An automobile-racing site, Brooklands, was turned into a major aviation center for research and development.

As the war continued, the Allies desperately needed a specially designed plane to retaliate against German bombing. The Vickers Aircraft Company responded by building a plane called the Vimy. But by the time the Vimy was ready, the war was over.

In peacetime the question was: could Vickers make this amazing new plane fly across the Atlantic? If they took out all the military equipment and fitted extra tanks, then the Vimy could carry enough fuel to extend its range to 2,440 miles (3,900 km)—well over the transatlantic distance. And they could reduce the crew space to hold two rather than three. . . .

All they needed was two brave and experienced aviators: a pilot and a navigator. They were lucky. They found John Alcock and Arthur Whitten Brown.

Aviator Louis Blériot was the first person to fly across the English Channel. He flew from Les Baraques, near Calais, to Dover without a compass. His success made people realize that the airplane might, in time, be used as a weapon of war.

Blériot's tiny monoplane had a wingspan of only 14 feet (4.3 meters).

The Bleriot Monoplane

3

ARTHUR WHITTEN BROWN

He was born in 1886. His parents were American, but he was brought up in Britain. When war broke out in 1914, he gave up his American citizenship to join the British Army. But he wanted to learn to navigate a plane and moved to the Royal Flying Corps. He escaped from one crash—his plane somersaulted over telegraph wires—only to be shot down and captured behind enemy lines. He was injured and was to be lame for life. A prisoner of war for two years, Brown studied aerial navigation—and dreamed of flying across the Atlantic.

JOHN ALCOCK

He was born in Manchester, England, in 1892. As a boy he flew model planes. As a young man he raced cars and motorbikes at Brooklands and learned to fly. When World War I began, he joined the Royal Naval Air Service, teaching cadets to be fighter pilots. Later he went to the Turkish front as an air scout. He became a record breaker for long-distance bombing raids—until he crashed into the sea and was captured by the Turks. He was their prisoner for over a year and spent much of this time thinking about freedom—and the Atlantic challenge.

• THE ADVENTURE BEGINS •

Alcock and Brown met by chance at Brooklands. Brown was looking for a job. Alcock had one, as a test pilot. Brown was determined to take up *The Daily Mail's* Atlantic challenge, and he saw in Alcock the partner he'd been looking for. Together they had the will and the necessary skills to go after the Atlantic prize. They began immediately. Alcock's job was to help adapt and test the Vimy No. 13. Brown concentrated on the apparatus and instruments to keep the plane on course.

They were not the only contenders. There was also a government-backed American team, with an A.V. Roe seaplane called the *Raymor*, to be flown by Raynham and Morgan. And Harry Hawker and Mackenzie-Grieve would fly a remodeled Sopwith bomber, the *Atlantic*.

The three friendly rival teams gathered on St. John's Island in Newfoundland between April and June, 1919. They chose to start from there as it is the closest point on the American continent to the British Isles, and they wanted to fly west-east because winds across the Atlantic blow from the west. The Vimy was taken apart, crated, and sent across on a cargo ship. Alcock, Brown, and their 10-man team went by passenger ship. Brown spent most of his time on the bridge, studying the Atlantic and its weather. As no one knew what the air conditions would be like, he took this chance to learn from the sea voyage. Now he knew that they could expect dense fog and storms violent enough to force an aircraft down!

Alcock and Brown's team arrived last at St. John's Island. Their rivals had already taken the ground most suitable for takeoff, and so a plan was needed. They employed 30 men to help them blow up rocks, remove walls, and level hills to clear a 400-yard (365-meter) runway.

The Vickers Vimy flew at about 118 mph.

It was bitterly cold. The team camped on site, making themselves sleeping and dining huts out of bits of the Vimy's crates.

On May 18, in spite of bad weather, Hawker and Grieve decided that they would be the first to go. They took off in the *Atlantic*. Two hours later, anxious to overtake the leaders, Raynham tried to take off, too. But the weather had deteriorated further. The *Raymor* was overloaded and crashed on takeoff.

Meanwhile, the *Atlantic* had been experiencing mechanical problems, mostly caused by icy weather, and had drifted off course. Hawker and Grieve eventually had to ditch the plane into the ocean. A small cargo ship picked them up, but because it had no radio, it was days before anyone knew they were safe.

Alcock and Brown, with the help of their team, had the difficult task of putting the Vickers Vimy together again after it arrived in Newfoundland. Theirs was the last plane to take off.

On June 9 and 12, Alcock made test flights and worked out last-minute problems. In view of the *Atlantic's* disastrous attempt, Alcock planned for a possible crash. The first fuel tank to be emptied could be turned into a life-saving raft. A supply of emergency rations was fitted into the tail and would be clear of the waves if the machine floated.

On Friday, June 13, Alcock had the oil, fuel, and water tanks filled. He and Brown went to bed at 7 P.M., hoping for an early start. The first two passengers destined to fly the Atlantic were already on board—their mascots, two toy cats. Lucky Jim had a huge head, an untidy ribbon, and a hopeful expression, but Twinkletoes' small face expressed surprise and anxiety.

Alcock and Brown were at the airfield by 3:30 A.M., but strong crosswinds made takeoff impossible. The engines were tested one last time. The food stores and Brown's navigational instruments went on board. Mailbags containing 300 private letters, specially stamped at St. John's, were loaded. The men waited for the weather to improve. In the afternoon they had their last meal under the wings of the aircraft. And then in spite of drizzling rain, Alcock decided to go.

Lord Northcliffe believed in nonstop transatlantic flight. The world watched as the first two challengers failed, leaving only Alcock and Brown.

Twinkletoes

Lucky Jim

9

As Alcock and Brown took their seats, a crowd gathered. Some shouted that the airmen would kill themselves before takeoff.

The Vimy had never flown with a full load before. Now it weighed 5 tons. Alcock had to take off uphill in the face of a 40-mph (64-kph) wind, from an airfield only 400 yards (366 meters) long. They moved forward, lurching over rough ground. A reporter from *The Times* watched them go:

"They slowly moved up the steep gradient . . . 100 yards–200 yards–300 yards and the machine still moved forwards, but showed not the least desire to leave the ground. . . . Suddenly and at just the right moment, Captain Alcock operated his control. . . . The machine jumped off the ground, zoomed over a fence which was just a few yards ahead, bounded over the eastern side of the aerodrome and began steadily to climb.

"For a moment there was silence—all but a few failed to realize that the machine was off on its journey . . . and then so loud a cheer was raised that it must have reached the airmen even against the gale. . . ."

Inside the Vimy, the fliers sat side by side, in their electrically heated suits. A high range of hills on either side made climbing difficult. A sudden eddy could turn the plane over. Brown held his breath in case the undercarriage hit a roof or treetop. Alcock was sweating heavily from anxiety—but his clever piloting saved the plane from an early disaster.

They flew over the airfield. Brown leaned over the side and waved. As they left the coast of Newfoundland, he looked back at the last buildings, fields, woods. . . . Their destination was Ireland. Between the two countries there was nearly 2,000 miles (3,200 km) of ocean. The two men were challenging science. No one had ever attempted to fly so high or so far before. Brown knelt on his seat to make observations. For the first hour he could see spots of blue sky and, below, the surface of a sea that contained more icebergs than friendly ships.

To find their position accurately, Brown would measure the angle that either the sun or a selected star made with the horizon.

In case the horizon was not visible, Brown had a spirit level, an instrument that told the aviator when his airplane was in an upright level position. At night or in thick clouds, the pilot would soon become completely disoriented. But, unlike Blériot, he did have a compass.

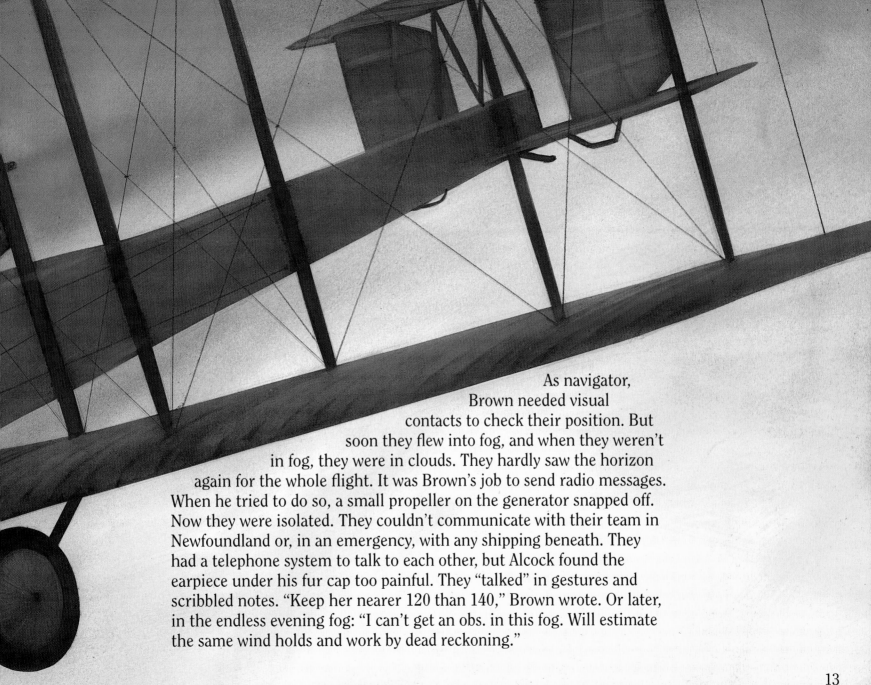

As navigator,
Brown needed visual
contacts to check their position. But
soon they flew into fog, and when they weren't
in fog, they were in clouds. They hardly saw the horizon
again for the whole flight. It was Brown's job to send radio messages.
When he tried to do so, a small propeller on the generator snapped off.
Now they were isolated. They couldn't communicate with their team in
Newfoundland or, in an emergency, with any shipping beneath. They
had a telephone system to talk to each other, but Alcock found the
earpiece under his fur cap too painful. They "talked" in gestures and
scribbled notes. "Keep her nearer 120 than 140," Brown wrote. Or later,
in the endless evening fog: "I can't get an obs. in this fog. Will estimate
the same wind holds and work by dead reckoning."

13

At six o'clock that evening, they were startled when the starboard engine began clattering like a machine gun. A chunk of exhaust pipe crumpled up and blew away. Three cylinders were sending exhaust fumes straight into the air. The men could see a flame licking from the open exhaust, and the roar was constant. At seven o'clock, Alcock went up to 2,000 feet (610 meters), trying to get above the clouds.

Moisture condensed on goggles, dial glasses, and wire. At 8:30, the sun appeared briefly through a gap in the upper clouds— just enough to project the shadow of the Vimy onto clouds below. Brown had long enough to make some calculations. Later he got a glimpse of the sea. He estimated that they were too far east and south.

By nine o'clock, the light was fading. Brown scribbled to Alcock, "Can you get above these clouds? . . . We must get stars as soon as pos."

Alcock climbed as steeply as he dared through the twilight. Now Brown could see only his luminous dials. He had to use an electric light to study his charts. He shined his flashlight over the side of the cockpit to inspect the engines. By 9:30, they were flying at 5,200 feet (1,585 meters), through dark clouds.

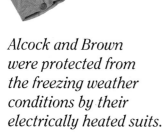

Alcock and Brown were protected from the freezing weather conditions by their electrically heated suits.

Brown waited impatiently for the first sight of the moon, the Pole Star—any star that would help him navigate.

They went higher and higher. . . . Suddenly, near midnight, Brown saw Vega and the Pole Star through a gap in the clouds and with them a cloud horizon defined in moonlight. Now he could use his sextant to fix their position. They had flown 850 nautical miles (1,574 km), at an average speed of 106 knots (196 kph), and were only slightly off course.

The moonlight was eerie as they flew toward dawn. Outside the cockpit it was bitterly cold.

Brown got snacks from the compartment above his head. Alcock ate with one hand. He never took the other one off the joystick, or his feet off the rudder bar, for the entire flight.

Five hours gone. . . . Another five hours. Ireland or . . . ?

Soon it would be sunrise (3:10 A.M.), but instead of sun they ran into dark clouds so dense that they couldn't see the ends of the plane. Jarring winds, hail, and sleet hit them. The Vimy flew wildly and began to perform circus tricks.

Both men lost all sense of balance, and there was no horizon to help get it back. They knew they were not flying level—but what was level? Which way was up?

Supplies included sandwiches, plenty of Fry's chocolate, Horlicks beverage, and hot Oxo in a Ferrostat thermos bottle.

FRY'S MILK CHOCOLATE

300 GOLD MEDALS & DIPLOMAS AWARDED TO THE FIRM

SIX-PENCE.

Alcock pulled back the control lever. The air speed meter jammed, and the engine stalled. The Vimy hung motionless for a second, its speed dropped, and suddenly it heeled over and fell into a spinning nose dive from 4,000 feet (1,220 meters). Alcock wrestled desperately with the controls, knowing only by the pressure on his back that they were rocking and falling. The compass swung wildly. They were dropping, 3,000—2,000—1,000—500 feet. If the cloud reached down to the sea, they might hit the water at any moment. The men loosened their safety belts, and Brown prepared to save the log of the flight.

Suddenly they spun out of the cloud. The ocean lay 100 feet below, at a strange tilted angle. A glimpse of the horizon restored Alcock's balance, and now only 50 feet from the sea—they could even hear the waves—he leveled the plane with a roar of the engines.

The Vimy rose, and when the compass had steadied itself, Brown realized that they were facing back toward America. He scribbled frantically to Alcock: "Immediately you see sun rising, point machine straight towards it, and we will get a compass bearing."

But there was no chance. More fog. More cloud. And now, rain, snow, sleet, vicious winds, and hail. . . .

No one had ever flown in such conditions before. Alcock kept climbing to get out of the weather and find an observation point for Brown. But climb as they might, they could not escape from the clouds. They went to 11,000 feet (3,350 meters), and it was so cold that ice covered the plane and frozen sleet jammed the flaps on the wings, which were meant to keep the plane flying level.

Lumps of snow covered the glass face of the fuel overflow gauge. Alcock needed to see it at all times in order to regulate the fuel supply to the engine. It was outside the cockpit, on one of the center section struts. There was just one thing to be done—and Brown, in spite of his lame leg, climbed out of his seat, holding a strut for support, to clear away the snow with a knife. The biting icy cold outside hit him, and a violent rush of air pushed him backward. Yet he managed to reach out and clear the snow several times during the hours of the terrible storm. Afterward, Brown said it hadn't been dangerous. But Alcock claimed that only Brown's amazing courage had saved their lives.

Brown kept a detailed logbook during the flight.

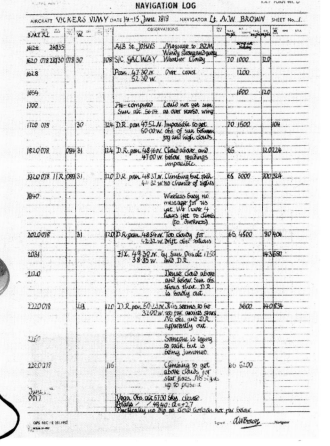

Long hours passed as they battled against the elements to keep the Vimy in the sky. And then, at last, a pinpoint of sun appeared. It was just enough for Brown to estimate (with his spirit level, since there was still no horizon) that they were nearing the Irish coast.

At 7:20 A.M. he wrote: "Better go down where air warmer . . . might pick up steamer. . . ."

Down at 1,000 feet, Brown saw the ocean surface and worked out their position for the first time since he had made his midnight calculations by the stars. They were well on course. Brown relaxed and got "breakfast" from the compartment. As he reached to put the thermos bottle back, Alcock grabbed his shoulder and pointed ahead to two specks of land. Then they were over ocean again—the land had disappeared.

Rain obscured the view. Later they learned that they had passed over the islands of Eashal and Turbot. At last the Irish mainland came into sight! It was 8:15 A.M., on June 15. Brown put away his charts. His work as navigator on the first transatlantic flight was over.

Several minutes later the tall masts of Marconi's Clifden Wireless Station appeared. Brown fired two red flares from his Verey pistol. No one saw them. The plane circled the village of Clifden. It was misty, and there was a danger that it might crash into high ground. Alcock decided to land in a field. He shut off the engines and glided toward it for a perfect landing. The wheels touched the earth and began to run smoothly over the surface. . . . Then the Vimy tilted, the tail rose, and, with a squish, the plane tipped forward and ended up as if it were trying to stand on its head.

They had landed in a bog but were not hurt. One of the propeller blades was buried in the ground. A connection broke, and fuel flooded into the rear cockpit. Alcock and Brown grabbed the mailbag and their instruments and scrambled out. Men from Marconi and Irish soldiers from Clifden rushed to help.

"Where are you from?" they asked.

"America." Everyone laughed. It was some time before Alcock convinced them it was true. He showed them the mailbag from St. John's—and they burst out cheering. Soon news of their arrival was going out in every direction.

They had been in the air for 16 hours, 28 minutes. They had flown 1,960 miles (3,154 km) at an average speed of over 2 miles (3.2 km) a minute and, in spite of all the hazards, landed almost on target.

"Very good going in the circumstances," Alcock said.

They were exhausted. This was the first case of "jet lag"—for they had overtaken time by more than three hours from sunset to sunset.

The plane landed in a bog. No one could believe they had actually made it!

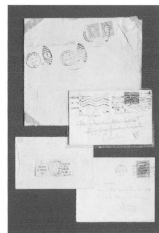

The letters from St. John's were delivered in London—the first transatlantic airmail!

23

The desire to fly goes back in time far beyond the Wright brothers or Alcock and Brown. Dreams of flight are recorded in ancient myths. Humans had to wait for the twentieth century for these dreams to come true.

News of Alcock and Brown's success was wired around the world. They returned to England by ship. They had won the race and were heroes!

The two airmen were met by representatives from *The Daily Mail* and Vickers—in particular the designer of the Vimy, Rex Pierson. Suddenly they were heroes, and it was flags, speeches, and crowds all around. They traveled by ship to England, and an airplane escorted their train to London, where they were carried shoulder high. At Euston Station the police had to lift Alcock into a car to rescue him from being mobbed.

Alcock delivered the first transatlantic airmail letters to the postal authorities, and at last the heroes had an evening off. Alcock went to a prizefight and Brown to see his girlfriend.

But honors were not over. The greatest celebrations took place, rightly, where the adventure had started—at Brooklands. Alcock showered praise on everyone who had had a part in building the Vimy. Most of all he praised Brown's skill as a navigator.

The Daily Mail check was presented to Alcock and Brown at the Savoy Hotel by Winston Churchill, then Secretary of War. He told them that they were commanded to go to Windsor Castle the next day, to be knighted by King George V.

Later the same year a Vimy was used when two Australians made the first flight from England to Australia. Ross and Keith Smith flew from Hounslow to Darwin in just under 28 days.

Alcock and Brown received their £10,000 ($50,000) prize from The Daily Mail. *The paper set many aviation challenges in the early twentieth century.*

At Windsor station there was a full civic reception. Then Alcock and Brown were driven to Windsor Castle in a royal carriage drawn by a pair of Windsor Greys. Eton school boys ran along by the side of the carriage, cheering and waving their top hats.

The two men were national heroes, and would surely be lifelong friends. . . . But six months later, on December 18, Alcock was flying a Viking Amphibian to the Paris Air Show. He was alone and there was thick fog. With no navigator to guide him, he got lost over France. Flying low to check his position, he crashed and died soon afterward.

Brown never got over the death of his friend. He never flew again. He died in 1948, aged 62. He had lived to see their historic journey prepare the way for regular transatlantic flight.

Besides the £10,000 ($50,000) that Alcock and Brown received from Associated Newspapers, they were also presented with 2,000 guineas (about $10,000) from the Ardath Tobacco Co. and a further £1,000 ($5,000) from a Mr. Lawrence Phillips.

Winston Churchill presented the Atlantic fliers with their prize.

As Alcock and Brown embarked upon their journey, they could not have known how significant their success would be. Their bravery paved the way to a new era—an age in which most destinations are just a flight away.

There is a statue at Heathrow Airport in memory of Alcock and Brown. And, in Ireland, the spot where they landed is now a well-known tourist attraction.

•Aviation History•

Transatlantic Firsts

Alcock and Brown made the first *nonstop* flight across the Atlantic on June 14-15, 1919. But a transatlantic flight in two stages had been completed three weeks before. Three American naval planes (Curtiss flying boats) had set off from Newfoundland. The pilots were intending to stop off on the midocean islands of the Azores. A storm forced down two of them, but the third managed to stay aloft and reached the Azores safely. After ten days the plane took off again and arrived in Lisbon, Portugal, on May 27.

The first solo crossing

In May 1927, the American Charles Lindbergh flew from New York to Paris in his monoplane *The Spirit of St. Louis*. He was the ninety-second person to have made the crossing, but he was the first to have done it solo. He won a prize of $25,000.

The first woman to fly across the Atlantic was American aviator Amelia Earhart. She was one of a crew of three in a Fokker, which made the crossing in June 1928. She made the flight solo in 1932.

The first scheduled commercial flights across the Atlantic, operated by Pan Am, began in June 1939.

Flight Times

• In 1919 Alcock and Brown made their transatlantic crossing in sixteen hours and 28 minutes.
• In 1952, an RAF Canberra crossed the Atlantic in both directions in a day. The outward flight took 3 hours and 25 minutes.
• In September 1975, Concorde crossed the Atlantic four times in one day.

If they could see us now

Alcock and Brown endured the cold, the wet, and the dark on their epic journey. Would they believe their eyes if they could see us now, enjoying in-flight food and entertainment, safely cocooned in a supersonic jet?

Now and then

Runways

To take off in their Vimy, Alcock and Brown needed a runway 1,198 feet long. A modern commercial jet, such as a Boeing 747, needs a runway of 11,155 feet.

Range

The Vimy's maximum range (in its specially lightened state) was 2,700 miles (4,345 km). The maximum range of a Boeing 747 is 6,000 miles (9,650 km).

SIZE

	Vimy	Boeing 747
Wing span	67.3 feet	195.9 feet
Length	42.6 feet	231.9 feet
Height	15.4 feet	63.3 feet

CAPACITY

The Vimy carried two men and two mascot cats. A Boeing 747 can accommodate 548 passengers plus crew members.

AVIATION RECORDS

	1919	1991
Speed	191 mph (308 kph)	4,534 mph (7,295 kph)
Altitude	34,600 ft (10,549 m)	354,110 ft (107,960 m)
Weight lifted	44,672 lb	1,322,754 lb

SPEED

The Vimy's average speed was 118 mph (190 kph). The maximum speed of the Boeing 747, at 30,000 feet (9,144 meters), is 612 mph (985 kph).

WOMEN AVIATORS

The first woman to be awarded a pilot's license—Aero-Club de France license number 36—was Elise Deroche, in March 1910. Later that year, America's first woman pilot, Blanche Scott, made her first solo flight.

Lilian Bland, having studied aircraft on display in England, designed, built, and piloted the first powered aircraft to fly in Ireland, in 1911. In that year also, the first flying school for women opened in France. In 1921 Bessie Coleman was the first African American woman to earn a pilot's license while training in France.

But of all the early women aviators, Amelia Earhart and Amy Johnson are probably the most famous.

Amelia Earhart

Amelia Earhart, born in Kansas in 1898, was the first woman to receive a pilot's license from the National Aeronautic Association in the United States. She set a world record in altitude and made many long-distance flights across America and the Atlantic. As one of a crew of three, she was the first woman to fly across the Atlantic in 1928. The flight took almost 25 hours, and they landed in Wales rather than Ireland, as planned!

In 1937 she began a round-the-world trip and on July 2 radioed that she was heading northeast across the Pacific from New Guinea. She and her navigator were not heard or seen again.

Amelia Earhart

Amy Johnson

Amy Johnson, born in Hull, England, in 1903, worked as a lawyer's secretary in 1936, earning money for flying lessons. In May 1930, she became one of the most famous women in the world by flying a Gypsy Moth biplane, solo, from England to Darwin, Australia. On the way, she made an emergency landing in the desert in the Middle East and, while she waited for a sandstorm to abate, sat under her plane with a drawn revolver to defend herself against wild dogs.

She went on to set many flying records before she died in 1941, when her plane ran out of fuel and crashed in the Thames estuary.

GLOSSARY

Altitude
The height of an object above a given level, usually sea level.

Biplane
An airplane with two sets of wings, one above the other.

Cockpit
An open compartment for the pilot in an aircraft's fuselage.

Flight plan
A written statement of route and procedures to be adopted.

Flyer
The Wrights' names for their powered airplanes.

Fuselage
The body or hull of an airplane.

Glider
An unpowered, heavier-than-air craft.

Hangar
A building for housing aircraft.

Looping the loop
Flying the airplane in a circular path within a vertical plane.

Port
To the left, or on the left-hand side of an aircraft.

Rudder
A vertical control surface used for guiding an aircraft.

Slipstream
The flow of air driven backward by the propeller.

Supersonic
Flight at speeds greater than the speed of sound.

Thrust
A force generated by the propeller or jet to propel the aircraft.

Wing
A plane's main lifting airfoil(s).

INDEX

PICTURE CREDITS

t-top   b=bottom   c=center   l=left   r=right

Hulton Deutsh Picture Company; 9, 23t, 30t, 30b.
Mary Evans Picture Library; 4.
Peter Newark Historical Pictures; 2, 3, 26r.
Robert Opic; 15b.
Popperfotos; 5, 24t, 25, 27l.
Quadrant Picture Library; 7.
Courtesy of the Royal Airforce Museum at
Hendon and Cardington; 9,11,14, 15t, 20c, 20l.
Science and Society Picture Library; 23b.

First published in the U.K. by
© 1996 Franklin Watts
Text © Carolyn Sloan
Illustrations © Simon Smith

Franklin Watts
96 Leonard Street
London
EC2A 4RH

Franklin Watts
14 Mars Road
Lane Cove, NSW
Australia

Editor: Rosemary McCormick & Kyla Barber
Designer: Eljay Crompton
Author: Carolyn Sloan
Artist: Simon Smith

Published by Silver Burdett Press in 1998

A Division of Simon & Schuster
299 Jefferson Road
Parsippany, New Jersey 07054-0480

Library of Congress Cataloging-in-Publication Data
Sloan, Carolyn
An incredible journey: the story of Alcock and Brown/by
Carolyn Sloan: illustrated by Simon Smith.
p. cm.—(An incredible journey)
Originally published: London, England: F. Watts, 1996.
Includes index.
Summary: An account of the first flight over the Atlantic
Ocean, from Canada to England, made in 1919 by John Alcock
and Arthur Whitten Brown.
1. Transatlantic flights—Juvenile literature. 2. Alcock, John,
Sir, 1892–1919—Juvenile literature. 3. Brown, Arthur,
Whitten, Sir, 1886–1948—Juvenile literature.
[1. Transatlantic flights. 2. Alcock, John, Sir, 1892–1919.
3. Brown, Arthur, Whitten, Sir, 1886–1948.] I. Smith,
Simon, ill. II. Title. III. Series.
TL531.S56   1998   97–7339
629.13'0911—dc21   CIP   AC

ISBN 0-382-39920-X (LSB)   10 9 8 7 6 5 4 3 2 1
ISBN 0-382-39921-8 (PBK)   10 9 8 7 6 5 4 3 2 1

Printed in Singapore